HOW TO
BE FILLED WITH
THE SPIRIT

by BILL BRIGHT

NOTES FOR TEACHERS

A Transferable Concept. Here at your fingertips is a tool that can be used to make disciples of each one in your group. A disciple? Yes. Someone who knows the principles Christ taught in His earthly ministry and has "transferred" or incorporated them into his or her own life. Thus, he has not only grown in the Lord himself, but he is also capable of transferring that concept (or principle) to another and helping him to also grow.

Growth is exciting. It's stimulating. Thought questions and Bible study questions are provided with each section in this booklet so that you have a place to start discussion and stimulate personal growth. This "how to" essential of the Christian life presents tremendous opportunities for teacher and students alike to revitalize their witness, reconsider their priorities and change their world.

Each section should take about 40-50 minutes of teaching time. But this is a general guideline. You can also tailor each lesson to the needs of the group. Students may want to incorporate their own thought questions and delve even deeper into Bible study.

Christians at all stages of maturity in the faith struggle at times. A clearer focus on what's really involved in the Christian walk encourages those who are growing weary in well-doing (often an indication of trying to live the Christian life by self-effort) and excites those who haven't really started walking wholeheartedly with the Lord. This booklet reaches those at all levels of Christian maturity and in every walk of life.

Renewing one's purpose or kindling the fires of faith—this booklet can do either or both.

WHAT IS A TRANSFERABLE CONCEPT?

When our Lord commanded the 11 men to whom He had most shared His earthly ministry to go into all the world and make disciples of all nations, He told them to teach these new disciples all that He had taught them (Matthew 28:18-20).

Later the apostle Paul gave the same instructions to Timothy: "...and the things which you have heard from me...these entrust to faithful men, who will be able to teach others also" (II Timothy 2:2).

In the process of counseling and interacting with tens of thousands of students, laymen and pastors year after year for almost 30 years, our staff have discovered that many church members, including people from churches which honor our Lord and faithfully teach His Word, are not sure of their salvation, that the average Christian is living a defeated and frustrated life and that the average Christian does not know how to share his faith effectively with others.

In our endeavor to help meet these three basic needs and to build Christian disciples, Campus Crusade for Christ, Inc. has developed a series of "how to's"—or "transferable concepts"—in which we discuss many of the basic truths that Jesus and His disciples taught.

A "transferable concept" may be defined as an idea or a truth which can be transferred or communicated from one person to another and then to another, spiritual generation after generation, without distorting or diluting its original meaning.

As these basic truths—"transferable concepts"— of the Christian life are made available through the printed word, films, tapes and cassettes in every major language of the world, they could well be used of God to help transform the lives of tens of millions all over the world.

We encourage you to master each of these concepts until you are personally prepared to communicate them to others "who will be able to teach others also." In so doing, many millions of men and women can be reached and discipled for Christ. They can then make a significant contribution toward the fulfillment of the Great Commission in our generation.

CONTENTS

Here's Life Publishers
P.O. Box 1576
San Bernardino, CA 92402

SECTION 1

INTRODUCTION

"My life will never be the same after tonight," commented the senior pastor of one of America's leading churches after he heard my message on "How to Be Filled With the Spirit." "I have been a pastor for more than 20 years," he said, "but

CHRIST-DIRECTED LIFE
† · Christ is in the life
  and on the throne
S · Self is yielding to Christ
• · Interests are directed
  by Christ, resulting in
  harmony with God's plan

have never understood how to be empowered and controlled by the Holy Spirit as a way of life until now. I can hardly wait to share this with my church members."

A retired businessman and his wife who had come to my office from halfway across the continent said, "Our lives were changed when we learned how to be filled with the Holy Spirit as a result of your ministry. Now we are sharing Christ with others wherever we go. We have come to ask you to share on television how to be filled with the Holy Spirit. Your simple approach reached us, and we want to help you reach multitudes of others."

Thousands of similar stories could be told of students, pastors and laymen who have made the exciting Scriptural discovery of how to be filled with the Holy Spirit by faith.

An Important Discovery

If you have not already done so, learning how to be filled with (controlled and empowered by) the Holy Spirit by faith will be the most important discovery of your Christian life.

Consider carefully the very last words of the Lord as He met with His disciples on the Mount of Olives only moments before He ascended into heaven. Jesus had commissioned His disciples to go into all the world and preach the gospel and to make disciples of all nations. But He had told

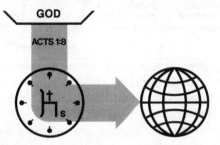

them not to leave Jerusalem *until they were filled with the power of the Holy Spirit.* "You shall receive power," He said, "when the Holy Spirit has come upon you; and you shall be My witnesses both in Jerusalem, and in all Judaea and Samaria, and even to the remotest part of the earth" (Acts 1:8).

By these words, Jesus was suggesting, "Though you have been with Me for three years and more, it is not enough that you have heard Me teach the multitudes, and have seen Me heal the sick and even raise the dead. You need to be empowered with the Holy Spirit if you are to be effective and fruitful as My witnesses throughout the world."

Power to Share

A very discouraged student came to me for counsel after one of my messages. For some months he had spent at least three hours each day reading his Bible, praying and sharing his faith with others. Yet, he had never introduced anyone to Christ. After a time of discussion, his problem became apparent — he was not controlled and empowered by the Holy Spirit, although he wanted to be.

So we prayed together, and by faith he appropriated the power of the Holy Spirit on the authority of God's Word. That very day he had his first experience of introducing a person to Christ. The next day he saw another come to Christ, and he has since introduced hundreds of people to the Lord. Obviously, his life was transformed.

A very successful businessman came to Arrowhead Springs, our International Headquarters, for training. The son of a minister, he had been reared under the good influence of the church, had been a Sunday school teacher for years, a Sunday school superintendent, a deacon, a member of the board of trustees of one of America's leading theological seminaries, and the president of all the laymen for his denomination for an entire state. Yet, he had never to his knowledge introduced anyone to Christ.

Multiplied Ministry

During the training he learned how to be filled with the Holy Spirit by faith and how to introduce others to Christ. Since that time, he has personally introduced hundreds of people to Christ and has trained thousands of laymen and pastors through our Lay Institutes for Evangelism. Thousands of others have been introduced to Christ through those whom he has trained.

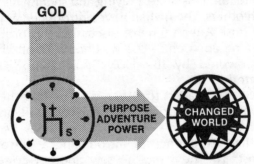

The pastor of a 1,500-member church appropriated the fullness of the Holy Spirit at a Pastor's Institute for Evangelism at Arrowhead Springs and learned how to introduce others to Christ. During one afternoon of witnessing for Christ, 14 of the 15 people whom this pastor interviewed received Christ.

Never before had he had such an experience. He returned to his pulpit a changed man. Soon hundreds of his church members, like their pastor, had appropriated the fullness of the Holy Spirit by faith. Now they are sharing their enthusiasm for Christ, and through their witness many more are responding to the Savior.

A Great Adventure

The Christian life is a great adventure. It is a life of purpose and power. Christ has given the almost unbelievable promise, "He who believes in Me, the works that I do shall he do also; and greater works than these shall he do; because I go to the Father. And whatever you ask in My name, that will I do. . ." (John 14:12,13).

Obviously, we cannot, in our own energy, accomplish these great works which He has promised we can do. It is Christ Himself — living within us, in all of His resurrection power, walking around in our bodies, thinking with our minds, loving with our hearts, speaking with our lips — who will empower us with the Holy Spirit to do these great works. It is not our wisdom, our eloquence, our logic, our good personalities, or our persuasiveness which brings men to the Savior.

It is the Son of Man, who came to seek and to save the lost. Jesus said, "Follow me and I will make you fishers of men" (Matthew 4:19). It is our responsibility to follow Him, and it is His responsibility to make us fishers of men. First-century Christians, controlled and empowered by the Holy Spirit and filled with His love, turned the world upside down.

As the disciples were filled with the Holy Spirit, they received a divine, supernatural power that changed them from fearful men into radiant witnesses for Christ. They were used of God to change the course of history. And that omnipotent power, the power of the Holy Spirit, is available to you, to enable you to live a holy and fruitful life for Jesus Christ.

Ignorance of the Holy Spirit

Yet, tragedy of tragedies, there are multitudes of Christians who do not even know who the Holy

Spirit is, or, if they do, they do not know how to appropriate His power. Consequently, they go through life without ever experiencing the abundant and fruitful life which Christ promised to all who trust Him.

Again and again I am reminded of the great contrast between Christ's church today and His church in the first century. In J. B. Phillips' introduction to the *Letters to the Young Churches,* he states:

"The great difference between present-day Christians and that of which we read in these letters (New Testament epistles), is that to us it is primarily a performance; to them it was a real experience. We are apt to reduce the Christian religion to a code, or, at best, a rule of heart and life. To these men it is quite plainly the invasion of their lives by a new quality of life altogether. They do not hesitate to describe this as Christ living in them."

First-Century Power

This same first-century power — the power of the risen, living, indwelling Christ made known through the Holy Spirit — is still available to us today. Do you know this power in your life? Are you a victorious, fruitful witness for Christ? If not, you can be.

For this reason, I believe the most important message that I could give to Christians is the wonderful news of the Spirit-filled life. I have shared these truths around the world with tens of thousands of Christians, old and young. No other message that I have shared has been used more by God to transform the lives of multitudes.

If you are not already experiencing the abundant life which Jesus promised and which is your heritage as a Christian, if you are not already introducing others to Christ as a way of life and you sincerely desire to do so, I have good news for you!

WHO, WHY, WHAT?

The answers to the following questions will lead you to a knowledge and experience of the Spirit-filled life: First, who is the Holy Spirit? Second, why did He come? Third, what does it mean to be filled with the Spirit? Fourth, why is the average Christian not filled with the Holy Spirit? Fifth, how can one be filled with the Holy Spirit?

The Holy Spirit is God. He is not an "it." He is not a divine influence, nor a fleecy white cloud, not a ghost nor a concept. He is God — with all the attributes of deity. He is the third person of the Trinity — co-equal with God the Father and God the Son. There is only one God, but He manifests Himself into three persons.

I cannot define the Trinity. No one can. One of my seminary professors once said, "The man who denies the Trinity will lose his soul. The man who tries to understand the Trinity will lose his mind." We who are finite cannot comprehend the infinite God.

We try to illustrate the concept of the Trinity, but the attempt is wholly inadequate. For example, I could say that a man has a body, a mind and a spirit — which one is the man? Or I could describe H_2O as a liquid, a solid or a vapor, depending on whether it was water, ice or steam. Which one is H_2O? Or a man is a husband, a father and a son — yet, he is one man. No illustration is adequate. At best, it can only suggest what the Trinity is like.

Why Did the Holy Spirit Come?

The Holy Spirit came to this earth to glorify Christ and to lead believers into all truth. On the eve of His crucifixion the Lord Jesus said to the disciples, "It is to your advantage that I go away; for if I do not go away, the Helper shall not come to you; but if I go, I will send Him to you. But when He, the Spirit of truth , comes He will guide you into all the truth. . .and He will disclose to you what is to come. He shall glorify Me; for He shall take of Mine and shall disclose it to you" (John 16:7,13,14).

The Holy Spirit came to enable us to know Christ, through the new birth, and to give us the power to live and share the abundant life which Jesus promised to all who trust Him.

Reveals Truth

The Holy Spirit inspired men to write the Holy Scriptures. As we read the Bible, He reveals its truth to us. I read passages of Scripture that I have read many times before, and suddenly, at the moment I need a particular truth, a certain passage comes alive to me. Why? Because the Holy Spirit makes the Word of God relevant and meaningful when I need it. It is a living Book inspired by the Spirit, and only the person who is controlled by the Spirit can understand the Bible (I Corinthians 2:10).

I pray, and — except for the prayer of confession — I cannot expect God to answer my prayer unless I am walking in the Spirit. I witness, and no one responds unless I am controlled by the Spirit.

A minister friend said to me, "I don't like all of this talk about the Holy Spirit. I want to talk about Jesus Christ." I reminded him that that was the reason the Holy Spirit came — to exalt and glorify Christ (John 16:1-15).

It is impossible even to know Christ apart from the regenerating ministry of the Spirit. It was Jesus of Nazareth Himself who said, "Unless one is born of water and the Spirit, he cannot enter into the kingdom of God" (John 3:5). It is impossible for us to pray, to live holy lives, to witness — there is nothing that we can do for the Lord Jesus and there is nothing that He can do for us — apart from the Holy Spirit of God.

What Does It Mean to be Filled With the Holy Spirit?

To be filled with the Holy Spirit is to be filled with Christ. Therefore, if I am filled with the Spirit, I am abiding in Christ. I am walking in the light as He is in the light (I John 1:7), and the blood of Jesus Christ will cleanse and keep on cleansing me from all unrighteousness (I John 1:9). I am controlled by Christ, because the word "filling" means to be controlled — not as a robot but as one who is led and empowered by the Spirit. And if I am controlled and empowered by Christ, He will be walking around in my body, living His resurrection life in and through me.

This amazing fact — that Christ lives in us and expresses His love through us — is one of the most important truths in the Word of God. The standards of the Christian life are so high and so impossible to achieve, according to the Word of

God, that only one person has been able to succeed. That person is Jesus Christ. Now, through His indwelling presence, He wants to enable all who will place their trust in Him to live this same supernatural life.

If we are willing to have Christ live His resurrection life in and through us, we will bear spiritual fruit — which includes the fruit of the Spirit and souls won to Him — as naturally as a healthy vine will bear an abundance of fruit. Jesus said in Mark 1:17, "Follow Me and I will make you become fishers of men." It is our responsibility to follow Christ — to abide in Him. It is His responsibility to make us fishers of men.

In John 15:8, He said, "By this is My Father glorified, that you bear much fruit, and so prove to be My disciples." One can be a great preacher, a Christian scholar, a deacon or elder, attend church meetings daily, live a clean, moral life, memorize hundreds of verses of Scripture, direct a church choir and teach Sunday school, but if he is not bearing fruit — if he is not introducing others to Christ as well as living a holy life, he is not filled with and controlled by the Holy Spirit, according to the Word of God.

How to Bear Spiritual Fruit

There are those who say, "I witness for Christ by living a good life." But, it is not enough to live a good life. Many non-Christians live fine, moral, ethical lives. According to the Lord Jesus, the only way that we can demonstrate that we are truly following Him is to produce fruit, which includes introducing others to our Savior as well as living holy lives. And the only way we can produce fruit is through the power of the Holy Spirit.

Some time ago I asked a leading theologian and dean of faculty for a renowned theological seminary if he felt that one could be a Spirit-filled person without sharing Christ as a way of life. His answer was an emphatic, "No!"

On what basis could he make such a strong statement? The answer is obvious. Our Savior came to "seek and to save the lost" (Luke 19:10), and He has "chosen and ordained" (John 15:16) us to share the good news of His love and forgiveness with everyone, everywhere. To be unwilling to witness for Christ with our lips is to disobey this command just as much as to be unwilling to witness for Him by living holy lives is to disobey His command. In neither case can the disobedient Christian expect God to control and empower his life.

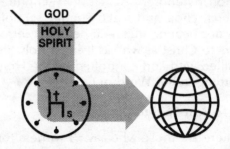

"I have been witnessing for years," a young man once said to me, "but have had no success. What is wrong with me?" After I explained how he could be filled with (controlled and empowered by) the Holy Spirit, we bowed to pray. By faith, he appropriated the fullness of God's Spirit, and immediately God began to use him to introduce others to the Savior.

Not only do we receive a natural power for witnessing when we are filled with the Spirit, but our personalities also begin to change. As we continue to walk in the control and power of the Holy Spirit, the fruit of the Spirit becomes increasingly obvious in our lives. In Galatians 5:22,23, Paul explains, "When the Holy Spirit controls our lives He will produce this kind of fruit in us: love, joy, peace, patience, kindness, goodness, faithfulness, gentleness and self control. . ." (Living Bible).

Critical and Progressive

The Christian's relationship with the Holy Spirit is both critical and progressive: critical, in that one learns that the Christian life is a life of faith rather than a life of works and that it has no reference to emotions ("The just shall live by faith" (Romans 1:17); progressive, in that as one walks consistently in the power and control of the Holy Spirit, the fruit of the Spirit will be produced in his life.

A word of caution is in order. Do not seek an emotional or mystical experience. Do not depend on mystical impressions. The Word of God must be the basis of our spiritual growth. There is an interesting parallel between the passage of Ephesians 5:18, which admonishes us to be constantly and continually directed and empowered by the Holy Spirit, and Colossians 3:16, which admonishes us to "let the Word of Christ richly dwell within you. . ."

The result of letting the Word of Christ dwell in us and being filled with the Holy Spirit will be our talking much about the Lord, quoting psalms and hymns and making music in our hearts to the Lord (Ephesians 5:19).

The Spirit Illumines the Word

It is very important that we recognize the importance of the balance between the Word of God and the Spirit of God. The Word of God is closed to our understanding and has little meaning to us apart from the illumination given by the Holy Spirit, and the Holy Spirit is hindered in speaking clear and life-changing truth apart from the Word of God.

When the emphasis on the ministry of the Holy Spirit and the Word of God is in proper balance in the believer's life, the result is a life of power and great fruitfulness in which our Savior, the Lord Jesus Christ, is wonderfully honored and glorified.

As we continue then to allow the Holy Spirit to control and empower us, and as we meditate upon the Word of God and hide it in our hearts, our lives express more and more the beauty of Christ and the fruit of the Spirit listed in Galatians 5:22,23. These attributes of our Lord Jesus Himself, plus fruitful witnessing, indicate that the Lord is actually living His life in and through us!

Obviously, then, being filled with the Spirit results in an abundant and overflowing life. Jesus of Nazareth once cried out to the multitudes, "If any man is thirsty, let him come to Me and drink. He who believes in Me, as the Scripture said, 'From his innermost being shall flow rivers of living water'" (John 7:37,38). John adds, "But this He spoke of the Spirit, whom those who believed in Him were to receive. . ." (John 7:39).

Truly, this is "the abundant life," yet most Christians are experiencing little of it.

Section 1

1. What command does God give in Ephesians 5:18 and what does it mean?

   _____

   _____

   _____

2. a) What characterizes the life of a Christian who is empowered by the Holy Spirit?

   _____

   _____

   b) How is the Holy Spirit's power evident in your own life?

   _____

   _____

3. Why did the Holy Spirit come?

   John 16:7,13,14 _____

   _____

   John 14:16,17,27 _____

   _____

4. How can you be filled with the Holy Spirit?

   _____

   _____

5. What does "fruit" mean in John 15:8?

   _____

   _____

6. If you were arrested for being a Christian, what evidence would there be to convict you?

_____

_____

_____

7. What does "the abundant life in Christ" mean to you?

_____

_____

_____

8. How do you witness to others?

_____

_____

_____

SECTION 2

APPROPRIATING THE FULLNESS

The average Christian continues to live in disobedience to God and is not filled with the Spirit for two reasons: first, a lack of knowledge; and second, unbelief.

Lack of Knowledge

I am persuaded that most non-Christians, if they knew how to become Christians and if they understood the exciting, adventurous life which the Lord gives to all who trust and obey Him, would become Christians. Can you conceive of an intelligent person saying "No" to Christ if he fully understood how much God loves him and that when he receives Christ his sins are all forgiven, he is given eternal life, and he receives a whole new life of meaning and purpose? A child of God is a person of dignity and destiny, and for him life is no longer a matter of mere existence.

But the non-Christian who lacks this knowledge continues to live in disobedience, rejecting God's love and forgiveness because he does not understand it. So it is with the carnal Christian. He continues to live a frustrated, fruitless life because he does not understand who the Holy Spirit is and what the rich, abundant and fruitful Christian life is all about — the life which awaits him when he invites the Holy Spirit to control and empower him.

From the moment of our spiritual birth, we have the power to go on growing toward maturity in Christ. And yet, the average person, not understanding how to live by faith, finds himself on a spiritual roller coaster, living from one emotional experience to another.

SELF-DIRECTED LIFE
S - Self is on the throne
† - Christ dethroned and not allowed to direct the life
• - Interests are directed by self, often resulting in discord and frustration

Legalistic attitude
Impure thoughts
Jealousy
Guilt
Worry
Discouragement
Critical Spirit
Frustration
Aimlessness

Ignorance of his spiritual heritage
Unbelief
Disobedience
Loss of love for God and for others
Poor prayer life
No desire for Bible study

In Romans 7, Paul describes the predicament of the carnal Christian, "For that which I am doing, I do not understand; for I am not practicing what I would like to do, but I am doing the very thing I hate. . . Wretched man that I am! Who will set me free from the body of this death?" (Romans 7:15,24).

The Carnal Christian

In I Corinthians 3, Paul describes a carnal Christian. Such a Christian is usually a miserable person — even more miserable than the non-believer. Having experienced the joy and blessing of fellowship with God, he has lost present contact and does not know how to recapture that lost fellowship. Yet, he can never be satisfied with that old way of life again, and in his search for happiness and fulfillment he has become self-centered instead of Christ-centered.

As a result, he has become increasingly confused and frustrated and does not know what to do about it. He does not know how to live by faith — he lives by feelings. He *tries* rather than *trusts*. He does not know how to stop being carnal, nor how to become a spiritual Christian. The only one who can enable him to change is, of course, the Holy Spirit.

Remember, the Lord Jesus said that we will do greater things than He did while He was here on this earth in His physical body. How is this to be accomplished? By the enabling power of the Holy Spirit.

Think of it! The Christian life is a miraculous life, a supernatural life. Christianity is not what we do for God, but what He does for us. Apart from faith in Christ, we cannot become Christians, and apart from moment-by-moment faith in dependence upon Him, we cannot live the Christian life. When we are filled with the Holy Spirit, Christ lives His supernatural life in and through us.

Living in Spiritual Poverty

But the average Christian does not understand how to draw upon the resurrection resources of Christ by faith. As a result he lives in spiritual poverty, not knowing or experiencing his great riches and resources in Christ.

In West Texas is a famous oil field known as the Yates Pool. During the depression, this field was a sheep ranch owned by a man named Yates. Mr. Yates was not able to make enough money on his ranching operation to pay the principal and interest on the mortgage, so he was in danger of losing his ranch. With little money for clothes or food, his family, like many others had to live on government subsidy.

Day after day, as he grazed his sheep over

those rolling West Texas hills, he was no doubt greatly troubled about how he would be able to pay his bills. Then a seismographic crew from an oil company came into the area and told Mr. Yates that there might be oil on his land. They asked permission to drill a wildcat well, and he signed a lease contract.

Resources Available

At 1,115 feet they struck a huge oil reserve. The first well came in at 80,000 barrels a day. Many subsequent wells were more than twice as large. In fact, 30 years after the discovery, a government test on one of the wells showed that it still had the potential flow of 125,000 barrels of oil a day. And Mr. Yates owned it all! The day he purchased the land he received the oil and mineral rights. Yet, he was living on relief. A multi-millionaire living in poverty! The problem? He did not know the oil was there. He owned it, but he did not possess it.

I do not know of a better illustration of the Christian life than this. The moment we become children of God through faith in Christ, we become heirs of God, and all of His resources are made available to us. Everything we need — including wisdom, love, power — to be men and women of God and to be fruitful witnesses for Christ — is available to us. But most Christians continue to live in self-imposed spiritual poverty, because they do not know how to appropriate from God those spiritual resources which are already theirs. Like Mr. Yates before the oil discovery, they live in ignorance of their vast riches.

Lack of Faith

Lack of knowledge is not the only reason that Christians are not filled with the Holy Spirit. There are many Christians who may have been exposed to the truth but who, for various reasons, have never been able to comprehend the love of God. They are afraid of Him! They simply do not trust Him.

Trust is another word for faith, and "without faith it is impossible to please God" (Hebrews 11:6). How would you feel if your child were to come to you and say, "Mother, Daddy, I don't love you. I don't trust you any more"? Can you think of anything that would hurt you more deeply? I cannot. And yet, by our attitudes and our actions, if not by our words, most of us say that to God. We live as though God did not exist, even though we give lip service to Him. We refuse to believe His promises that are recorded in His Word.

Many people are afraid to become Christians for fear that God will require the impossible of them — that He will change their plans, require them to give away their wealth, take all the fun from their lives, make them endure tragedies, or something similar.

An outstanding young minister, a seminary honor graduate, once told me, "I have never surrendered my life to Christ because I have been afraid of what He will do to me." Then he told me how, years before, he had had a premonition that if he were to commit his life to Christ, his parents would be killed in a tragic accident. He was afraid to say "Yes" to God for fear his parents would lose their lives — God's test for him to determine the genuineness of his commitment.

You Can Trust God

Now does that sound like a loving Father? Who do you think put that idea into his mind? Certainly not God. It was Satan saying, as he said to Adam and Eve centuries ago, "You can't trust God." But I say you can trust God! He loves you and is worthy of your trust.

Suppose my two sons were to greet me with these words: "Dad, we love you and we have decided that we will do anything you want us to do from now on as long as we live." What do you think would be my attitude?

If I were to respond to their expression of trust in me as many believe God will respond when they surrender their lives to Him, I would take my sons by the shoulders, shake them, glare at them sternly and say, "I have been waiting for this. I am going to make you regret this decision as long as you live. I am going to take all the fun out of your lives — give away your possessions and make you do all of the things you do not like to do."

Of course, I would never respond in that manner. If my sons came to me with such a greeting, I would put my arms around them and say, "I love you, too, and I deeply appreciate this expression of your love for me. It is the greatest gift which you could give me."

God Loves You

Is God any less loving and concerned for His

children? No, He has proven over and over again that He is a loving God. He is worthy of our trust. Jesus assures us, "If you then, being evil, know how to give good gifts to your children, how much more shall your Father who is in heaven give what is good to those who ask Him" (Matthew 7:11).

Many students and adults come to me for counsel concerning God's will for their lives. Often they are fearful of what God will ask them to do. Usually I ask them, "Do you believe that God loves you? Do you believe that He has a wonderful plan for your life? Does He have the power to guide and bless your life if you place your trust in Him?"

As a rule, the answers are in the affirmative. I then ask them, "Are you willing to trust Him right now to direct and empower you to live a holy life and to be a fruitful witness for Christ?" By this time most of them are ready to say "Yes" to Him without reservation. They have begun to recognize that their feelings of doubt have been placed there by the enemy of their souls.

Blessing in Return

When you give your life to Christ, you need not worry about what is going to happen to you. Maybe you are afraid that He will take away your pleasures, cause you to leave your business or profession, take away your wealth, or terminate a friendship or love affair. You may fear that He will send you as a missionary to some remote part of the world where you will lose your life for Him.

He may indeed ask you to do one or more of these things, and again He may not. If He does, you will rejoice in the privilege, for God always blesses those who trust and obey Him. Some of the happiest people I have ever met are serving Christ in remote, primitive parts of the world. Others have given up fame and fortune to follow Him. The Bible reminds us, "The eyes of the Lord run to and fro throughout the whole earth to make Himself strong in behalf of those who love Him, whose hearts are perfect toward Him" (II Chronicles 16:9).

You can trust God. If He leads you to give up anything, He will give you more of His blessing in return than you would ever receive apart from His grace. God alone is worthy of your trust. I invite you to come freely to Christ and say, "Lord, here I am. Take my life and use me for Your glory."

You need not fear what He will do to you. As God reminds us in I John 4:18, "We need have no fear of someone who loves us perfectly; His perfect love for us eliminates all dread of what He might do to us. If we are afraid, it is for fear of what He might do to us, and shows that we are not fully convinced that He really loves us." The Word of God and the experiences of multitudes through the centuries give unqualified assurance that we can trust God with our lives, our all.

We are filled with the Holy Spirit by faith. How did you become a Christian? By faith. "For by grace you have been saved through faith; and that not of yourselves, it is the gift of God; not as a result of works, that no one should boast"

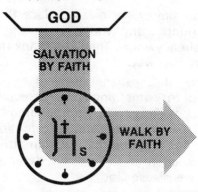

(Ephesians 2:8,9). As you therefore have received Christ Jesus the Lord, so walk in Him" (Colossians 2:6).

We received Christ by faith. We walk by faith. Everything we receive from God, from the moment of our spiritual birth until we die, is by faith. Do you want to be filled with the Holy Spirit? You can be filled right now, wherever you are, by faith.

You do not have to beg God to fill you with His Holy Spirit. You do not have to barter with Him, by fasting or weeping, or begging or pleading. For a long period of time, I fasted and cried out to God for His fullness. Then one day I discovered from the Scriptures that the "just shall live by faith" (Galatians 3:11). We do not earn God's fullness. We receive it by faith.

Suppose that you want to cash a check for a hundred dollars. Would you go to the bank where you have several thousand dollars on deposit, place the check on the counter, get down on your knees and say, "Oh, please, Mr. Teller, cash my check"? No, that is not the way you cash a check. You simply go in faith, place the check on the counter, and you wait for the money which is already yours. Then you thank the teller and go on your way.

Millions of Christians are begging God, as I once did, for something which is readily available — just waiting to be appropriated by faith. They are seeking some kind of emotional experience, not realizing that such an attitude on their part is an insult to God — a denial of faith, by which we please God.

Heart Preparation

Though you are filled with the Holy Spirit by faith and faith alone, it is important to recognize that several factors contribute to preparing your heart for the filling of the Holy Spirit.

First, you must desire to live a life that will please the Lord. We have the promise of our Savior, "Blessed are those who hunger and thirst for righteousness for they shall be filled" (Matthew 5:6).

Second, be willing to surrender your life to Christ in accordance with the command of God revealed in Romans 12: "And so, dear brothers, I plead with you to give your bodies to God. Let them be a living sacrifice, holy — the kind He can accept. When you think of what He has done for you, is this too much to ask? Don't copy the behavior and customs of this world, but be a new and different person with a fresh newness in all you do and think. Then you will learn from your own experience how His ways will really satisfy you" (Living Bible).

Confess Each Sin

Third, confess every known sin which the Holy Spirit calls to your remembrance and experience the cleansing and forgiveness which God promises in I John 1:9 : "But if we confess our sins to Him, He can be depended on to forgive us and to cleanse us from every wrong. And it is perfectly proper for God to do this for us because Christ died to wash away our sins" (Living Bible).

If you have wronged a brother, or have taken that which is not rightfully yours, the Holy Spirit may lead you to make restitution — to right your wrong. If so, obey Him or you will miss His blessing. The blessings of the fullness of God's Spirit come only to those who willingly obey Him.

Jesus promised, "The person who has My commands and keeps them is the one who really loves Me, and whoever really loves Me will be loved by My Father. And I too will love him and will show Myself to him. . .I will make Myself real to him" (John 14:21).

Again, we are not filled with the Holy Spirit because we desire to be filled, nor because we confess our sins or present our bodies a living sacrifice — we are filled by faith. These are only factors which contribute toward preparing us for the filling of the Spirit by faith.

Command and Promise

There are two very important words to remember. The first is *command.* In Ephesians 5:18 God commands us to be filled: "Be not drunk with wine, wherein is excess, but be filled with the Spirit." Not to be filled, controlled and empowered by the Holy Spirit is disobedience. The other word is *promise* — a promise that makes the command possible: "This is the confidence which we have before Him that, if we ask anything according to His will, He hears us. And if we know that He hears us in whatever we ask, we know that we have the requests which we have asked from Him" (I John 5:14,15).

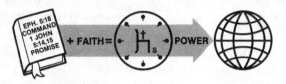

Now, is it God's will for you to be filled and controlled by Him? Of course it is His will — for it is His command! Then right now you can ask God to fill you — not because you deserve to be filled, but on the basis of His promise.

If you are a Christian, the Holy Spirit already dwells within you. Therefore, you do not need to invite Him to come into your life. He did this when you became a Christian and Jesus promised that He will never leave you (Hebrews 13:5). The moment you received Christ, the Holy Spirit not only came to indwell you, but He also imparted to you spiritual life, causing you to be born anew as a child of God. The Holy Spirit also baptized you into the Body of Christ. In I Corinthians 12:13, Paul explains, "For by one Spirit we are all baptized into one body."

There is but one indwelling of the Holy Spirit, one rebirth of the Holy Spirit and one baptism of the Holy Spirit — all of which occur when you receive Christ. Being filled with the Holy Spirit, however, is not a once-and-for-all experience. There are many fillings, as is made clear in Ephesians 5:18. In the Greek language in which this command was originally written, the meaning is clearer than that in most English translations. This command of God means to be constantly and continually filled, controlled and empowered with the Holy Spirit as a way of life.

If you wish to be technical, you do not need to pray to be filled with the Holy Spirit, as there is no place in Scripture where we are commanded to pray for the filling of the Holy Spirit. We are filled by faith. However, since the object of our faith is God and His Word, I suggest that you pray to be filled with the Spirit as an expression of your faith in God's command and in His promise. You are not filled because you pray, but because by faith you trust God to fill you with His Spirit.

What a relief it was to me one day when I read in Romans 8, "The old sinful nature within us is against God. It never did obey God's laws and it never will" (Romans 8:7). I had been trying to make myself good enough to please God, and that is impossible. The Bible says, "The heart is deceitful above all things, and desperately wicked" (Jeremiah 17:9). Therefore, I cannot hope to make myself good enough to earn God's favor. The only way I can please God is through faith. Paul talks about this concept in his letter to the Galatians: "I have been crucified with Christ; and it is no longer I who live, but Christ lives in me; and the life which I now live in the flesh I live by faith in the Son of God, who loved me, and delivered Himself up to me" (Galatians 2:20).

New Master — New Life

The individual who walks by faith in the control of the Spirit has a new Master. The Lord Jesus said, "If anyone wishes to come after Me, let him deny himself and take up his cross, and follow Me" (Matthew 16:24). "Unless a grain of wheat falls into the earth and dies, it remains by itself alone; but if it dies, it bears much fruit" (John 12:24).

Obviously, I cannot control myself and be controlled by the Holy Spirit at the same time. Christ cannot be in control if I am on the throne. So I must abdicate. This involves faith. As an expression of my will, in prayer, I surrender the throne of my life to Him, and by faith I draw upon His resources to live a holy and fruitful life.

The command of Ephesians 5:18 is given to all believers to be filled, directed and empowered by the Holy Spirit, continually, every day of our lives. And the promise of I John 5:14,15 is made to all believers that, when we pray according to God's will, He hears and answers us. If you pray to be filled with God's Spirit, He will hear and answer you. He will fill you.

Do Not Depend Upon Feelings

Do not think that you have to have an emotional experience or that something dramatic must happen to you. How did you receive Christ? Was it because of some emotional pressure brought to bear upon you? Your emotions may have been involved, but ultimately you became a Christian, not because of your emotional experience, but because of your faith. The Bible says, "For by grace you are saved by faith" (Ephesians 2:8).

The emotional experience was a by-product of an expression of faith or of an act of obedience. The Holy Spirit is not given to us that we might have a great emotional experience, but that we might live holy lives and be fruitful witnesses for Christ. So, whether or not you have an emotional experience is not the issue.

Have you met God's conditions? Do you hunger and thirst after righteousness? (Matthew 5:6) Do you sincerely desire to be controlled and empowered by the Holy Spirit? If so, I invite you to bow your head and pray this prayer of faith right now. Ask God to fill you. Without begging or pleading, just say:

"Dear Father, I need You. I acknowledge that I have been in control of my life and that, as a result, I have sinned against You. I thank You that You have forgiven my sins through Christ's death on the cross for me. I now invite Christ to take control of the throne of my life."

"Fill me with the Holy Spirit as You commanded me to be filled and as You promised in Your Word that You would do if I asked in faith. I pray this in the authority of the name of the Lord Jesus Christ. As an expression of my faith, I now thank You for filling me with Your Holy Spirit and for taking control of my life."

If this prayer expressed the desire of your heart, you can be sure that God has answered it. You can begin this very moment to draw upon the vast, inexhaustible resources of the Holy Spirit to enable you to live a holy life and to share the claims of the Lord Jesus and His love and forgiveness with people everywhere.

Remember that being filled with the Holy Spirit is a way of life. We are commanded to be constantly controlled by the Holy Spirit. Thank Him for the fullness of His Spirit as you begin each day, and continue to invite Him to control your life moment by moment. This is your heritage as a child of God.

Filled to Share

The primary purpose for which we are filled with the Holy Spirit is to make us witnesses for Christ through the life that we live and the words which we speak. Remember our Lord's final words to His disciples, and through them to us: "You shall receive power when the Holy Spirit has come upon you; and you shall be My witnesses both in Jerusalem, and in all Judea and Samaria, and even to the remotest part of the earth" (Acts 1:8).

The greatest spiritual awakening since Pentecost has, in my opinion, already begun. Millions of Christians are discovering this great source of power which altered the course of history and turned a wicked Roman Empire upside down. That same power, the power of the Holy Spirit, is being released through the lives of believing and obedient Christians in our generation to turn our world around and accelerate the fulfillment of the Great Commission in our generation.

Remember, "How to Be Filled with the Holy Spirit" is a transferable concept. I encourage you to master it and to begin to "teach these great truths to trustworthy men who will, in turn, pass them on to others" (II Timothy 2:2, Living).

Section 2

1. Why is the average Christian not living in complete obedience to God?

   _____

   _____

   _____

2. Make a list of the priorities in your life right now. What place does *self* have in each?

   _____

   _____

   _____

3. How do these verses describe the riches of Christ?

   Romans 2:4 _____

   _____

   Romans 9:23 _____

   _____

   Romans 11:33 _____

   _____

Ephesians 1:7 _____

_____

Ephesians 3:8 _____

_____

Hebrews 11:26 _____

_____

4. Romans 8:16,17 says that we are joint-heirs with Christ. In light of the above answer, what does that relationship mean to you?

_____

_____

_____

5. a) What promises of God have you claimed?

_____

_____

_____

_____

b) How has claiming them made a specific difference in your life?

_____

_____

_____

6. What do these verses tell you about God's love for you?

Matthew 7:11 _____

_____

John 10:28 _____

_____

II Chronicles 16:9 _____

_____

John 14:21 _____

_____

Hebrews 13:5 _____

_____

7. How is the command of Ephesians 5:18 related to the promise of I John 5:14,15? How can this give you assurance that you are filled with the Holy Spirit?

_____

_____

_____

_____

STUDY GUIDE

1. Read this booklet and/or listen to the cassette tape of this concept for six consecutive days. Educational research has shown that it is necessary to read or hear a concept six to ten times in order to understand it thoroughly. Think through the questions at the end of each section each time you read the concept. As you apply the principles presented in this concept, being filled with the Holy Spirit will become a way of life for you. A thorough understanding of this concept will enable you to communicate it more effectively to others.

2. Memorize the following verses and references:

   Ephesians 5:18: "And do not get drunk with wine, for that is dissipation, but be filled with Spirit."

   I John 5:14,15: "And this is the confidence which we have before Him, that if we ask anything according to His will, He hears us. And if we know that He hears us in whatever we ask, we know that we have the requests which we have asked of Him."

   Your memory work will be easier and more lasting if you will review it daily for the entire week rather than try to complete it in just one day. Also review the verses you memorized in previous Concepts.

3. Work the review questions at the end of each section, looking up the Scripture references and filling in the blanks with your answers.

4. Participate in a group discussion using the Bible study. If you are not already a part of a Bible study or some other group that is studying the Transferable Concepts, you can form your own group by inviting others to join you in this study program. As you discuss the Bible study questions, share what God is teaching you about being filled with the Holy Spirit and how you plan to apply this teaching in your life.

5. Finally, make this Concept, "How to Be Filled With the Spirit," a way of life by practicing the following:

    a. Set aside special time to be alone with the Lord each day. Be sure that our Lord Jesus Christ is in control of your life and that you are filled with the Holy Spirit as you begin each day. Thank God for what He is going to do in your life and for the way He is going to use you in the lives of others. Ask Him to lead you to those who are in need of Christ's love and forgiveness.

    b. Make a practice of breathing spiritually each time you become aware of the need. Simply exhale by confessing your sin and inhale by appropriating the fullness of the Holy Spirit by faith.

    c. Use the brief outline in the front of this booklet, the amplified outline in the back, or a tape recording of this Concept as a means of sharing this vital truth with other people. Share it as often as you can throughout the week. Provide a booklet, and perhaps a tape or cassette, for those with whom you share this Concept so that they, too, can study this material in depth and pass it on to others.

AMPLIFIED OUTLINE

A. Learning how to be filled (controlled and empowered) with the Holy Spirit is the most important discovery of the Christian life.

   1. You can experience the abundant life Jesus promised.

   2. You can introduce others to Christ.

B. Even though they had been with the Lord for three years, the disciples were not equipped to carry out the Lord's Great Commission until they were filled with the Holy Spirit (Acts 1:4,8).

C. Jesus promised that we would do greater works than He did (John 14:12-14).

   1. Obviously we cannot accomplish these greater works ourselves.

   2. They will result from the Son of Man, who came to seek and to save the lost, working through us.

   3. Our responsibility is to follow Christ; His responsibility is to make us fishers of men (Matthew 4:19).

   4. The same power received by the disciples at Pentecost — when they were filled with the Holy Spirit — which enabled them to change the course of history is available to us.

D. Tragically, multitudes of Christians do not know how to be filled with the Spirit.

I. Who is the Holy Spirit?

   A. He is God.

   B. He is the third person of the Trinity, co-equal with God the Son.

Why did the Holy Spirit come?

   A. He came to glorify Christ and to lead us into the truth of God's Word (John 16:13,14).

   B. He guides us in our prayer life.

   C. He gives us power to witness (Acts 1:8).

   D. It is impossible to even know Christ apart from the Spirit (John 3:5).

III. What does it mean to be filled with the Holy Spirit?

   A. To be filled with the Holy Spirit is to be filled with Christ and to be abiding in Him (John 15:1-8).

   B. Being filled with the Spirit has a twofold significance.

      1. We will bear spiritual fruit.

         a. Christ, who "came to seek and to save the lost," will, through the power of the Holy Spirit, produce through us the fruit of souls won to the Lord (John 15:16, Matthew 4:19).

         b. As the Holy Spirit controls us, we will mature in Christ and the fruit of the Spirit will become increasingly evident in our lives (Galatians 5:22,23).

    2. The Word of God will become more meaningful to us.

        a. God's Word is the basis of our spiritual growth (Colossians 3:16).

        b. The Holy Spirit illumines and applies the Word.

IV. Why is the average Christian not filled with the Holy Spirit?

    A. The average Christian continues to live in defeat and is not filled with the Spirit because of lack of knowledge.

        1. If he knew how much God loved him and the power that was available to him to experience an abundant life, the carnal Christian would no more want to remain carnal than the non-Christian would want to remain a non-Christian.

        2. He does not understand that from the moment of spiritual birth God has made His power available to enable the Christian to go on growing toward maturity in Christ.

        3. The average Christian, not understanding how to be filled with the Spirit by faith, lives a miserable, defeated, roller coaster kind of life Romans 7:15,25).

        4. The average Christian is not aware of his spiritual heritage.

    B. The average Christian is not filled with the Spirit because of unbelief.

1. Many people are afraid of God; they do not trust Him (Hebrews 3:19, I John 4:18).

2. Many feel that God will require the impossible of them; they doubt the extent of God's love (Matthew 7:11).

3. Many feel that God will take away their pleasures; they do not realize how great is His plan for us (Matthew 6:33).

V. How can you be filled with the Holy Spirit?

  A. You are filled with the Spirit by faith.

    1. You become a Christian by faith (Ephesians 2:8,9).

    2. You also walk in the Spirit by faith (Colossians 2:6).

  B. You do not have to beg God for what is already yours (Romans 1:17).

  C. Several factors contribute to heart preparation for being filled by faith.

    1. You must desire to live a life that will please the Lord (Matthew 5:6).

    2. You must be willing to surrender the control of your life to Christ according to the command of God (Romans 12:1,2).

    3. You must confess any sin which the Holy Spirit calls to your remembrance and claim His forgiveness (I John 1:9).

  D. There are two words to remember in claiming His filling by faith.

    1. His command is that we be filled with the Spirit (Ephesians 5:18).

2. His promise is that He always answers when we pray according to His will (I John 5:14,15).

E. It is important to remember:

1. If you are a Christian, the Holy Spirit already indwells you.

2. Being filled with the Holy Spirit is not a once-and-for-all experience; we are to be constantly filled with the Holy Spirit as a way of life.

3. It is not simply by prayer that we are filled. It is by faith.

F. We can never make ourselves good enough to please God; we must live by faith (Romans 8:7; Jeremiah 17:9; Galatians 2:20).

G. The result of being filled and of walking in the Spirit is that we become dead to self and alive to God (Matthew 6:24; John 12:24).

H. We live by faith. Feelings are valid as a by-product of faith and obedience, but at no time should we depend upon feelings alone.

These Transferable Concepts are designed to make an important contribution toward your spiritual growth, but they are no substitute for the Word of God. If you do not already have a regular time when you study the Bible, we encourage you to begin one. To help you get started, a brief outline that you may want to use in your study follows. Simply select a short passage of Scripture and use the next four steps:

Observation. What do you see in this passage of Scripture? What does it tell you?

Interpretation. What does it mean?

Application. How can you use this in your life? What steps are needed to put this into practice?

Correlation. How does it fit in with other Scripture verses? (It is important to keep sections of Scripture in context with the entire scope of the chapter or book.)